CW00972030

SONGBOOK: COLLECTED WORKS

Joshua Idehen is a British-born Nigerian based in Sweden. A spoken word artist, musician and facilitator, he has contributed poems to Mercury-nominated albums *Channel The Spirits* by The Comet Is Coming, *Your Queen Is A Reptile* and the Mobo-winning *Black To The Future*, both by Sons of Kemet. More recently, he worked with LA electronic maestro Daedelus on the critically acclaimed mini LP, *Holy Water Over Sons*. In 2023, he continued his journey as a solo musical artist, collaborating with producer Ludvig Parment (Saturday, Monday) on his mixtape *Learn To Swim*, released to critical acclaim and support, leading to a performance in front of the King of Sweden and (more importantly) Angelique Kidjo at the 2023 Polar Prize Award show (TV4). This is his first book.

INCLUDING POETRY FEATURED ON...

Learn to Swim, a Mixtape
Joshua Idehen, 2023

Bone and Soil - Shabaka Hutchings Remix
Chelsea Carmichael, 2022

Glass Effect
Ben Marc, 2022

Black to the Future
Sons of Kemet, 2021

Holy Water Over Sons
Daedelus, Joshua Idehen 2021

Your Queen Is A Reptile
Sons of Kemet, 2018

Last Night
Benin City, 2018

Fires In the Park
Benin City, 2013

38 EP
LV, Joshua Idehen, 2012

Songbook: Collected Works

JOSHUA IDEHEN

BAD BETTY PRESS

First published in 2024 by Bad Betty Press
Cobden Place, Cobden Chambers, Nottingham NG1 2ED

badbettypress.com

PB ISBN: 978-1-913268-60-2
EPUB ISBN: 978-1-913268-61-9

A CIP record of this book is available from the British Library.

Cover artwork by Gaurab Thakali
Interior images by Jenny Matthews, Valeriya Potapova and
Pictorial Press Ltd via Alamy Stock Photo
Book design by Amy Acre

Printed and bound in the UK by TJ Books Limited, Padstow, Cornwall
using FSC® Certified paper from responsibly managed forests

To Birdsong

CONTENTS

Songbook: Collected Works

WE'RE ALL FIELD NEGROES NOW

I am a field negro now, exodusing
from wretched plains. Pour holy palm
wine, wash away the shame

Blood is thicker
than sugar cane

I don't think you're ready for the pain
I don't think you're ready for the change

You are a field negro too, son. Leave
Candace Owens on the plantation

Foolish us, thinking the overseer
had the keys to these chains, the dungeon keeper
would play this game fair

Oh, bless your greed, for not
granting me the little I asked
of you

I would have played
the fiddle and tap danced
for you

I would have settled
for some Skittles and a safe
path home

tightened up my belts,
lightened up my skin, bitten down
my tongue.

I begged you for an inch
let me have some liquor
and a flatscreen, a minute
for my mind, scraps
for my sandwich.

You had me saying prayers
in your language, made me forget
my gods, question my spirits
forsake my prophets and then
you cursed me with Trevor Phillips

Oh, the pale-faced cheek of it

One knee on my
neck, one knee
on my lungs telling me to run
sprint times
on a marathon, keep calm
and carry on! Oh the audacity,

the caucasity of it all

Thank you for refusing me
that inch, because now I do not recognise
your yardstick. The scales have toppled,

the curtains have collapsed, the blonde baboon's
arse is bare in the open

I am a field negro now!
I do not want your equality!
it was never yours
to give, and even that
is too minor, too
little, too late!

Pull the balaclava
over my heart and
set it running!

My revolution rides
atop a black horse
and it is stunning!

Gather me my flowers, shower
them over my escape
route. Molotov cocktails
as my banner, skull and
crossbones is my skin
tone. Babylon burn down
is my jam, mate, my ringtone!

We are rolling your monuments
across the street like tobacco, tossing
your effigies into the river, weren't
even worth a pyre

Let me show you
what you've taught me
about crimes,
forget a piece we want the
pie and the *Everything
Must Go* sign

We're all field negroes now,
dead this talk, get me my bag

maybe one day we'll see eye to
eye on fancy furniture but
right now tho? sorry not sorry

burnitall

Field Negus. Sons of Kemet. Idehen, Joshua.
Black to the Future. Impulse! 2021

EPITAPH FOR TAMIR RICE

What's the market price for a black life?

Epitaph for Tamir Rice

Toss could-have-beens down wishing wells
this strange fruit was only twelve

Sunday dreams for a would-be teen
strutting free on hungry streets

basic rhymes on Logic beats
pocket full of sticky sweets

Cheeky grins and childish sins
skipping class to chill with kin

oily-faced on chicken wings
horizon still holds brighter things

Obsessing over TikTok dances
3-point miss and second chances

juicy lust and second glances
straight-up dissed, brethren laughing

Drunken uncles couched on porches
horror stories from the forties

back then it was horses and torches
now they got cars and badges
Reaper said *you're too young bro*
should be home on your console
bullet holes right through your torso

                              I had a dream I was haunted
                              no way I could stop it

Gazebo held those final scenes
winter's snow carpets the greens

said he looked old for his jeans
black boys often look like fiends

Pellet gun belonged to friends
he borrowed someone else's end

someone else's sis in cuffs
some other mother's heart in knots

What could have been, what could have been?
parking tickets, nothing more

screwface over evening chores
Miseducation or The Score

The ones who could have made you blush
backseat eyes and cold blood rush

Ghana trip to see the wonders
beach party with brand new brothers

Smiling like a summer god
we find our joy against the odds

holy water over sons
holy water

Haunted. Daedelus. Idehen, Joshua. Dove Dixon, Katie.
Holy Water Over Sons. Albert's Favourites, 2021

RIVER NIGER TO THE COLONISER

You might be made of mostly water
but I am wholly water

you are not the same as I
say your name into my belly

and your mouth will come back dry
I will not wash that dirty tongue

stare into my bosom, find no reflection
Child of Noah, I am descended

from the flood. I saw your fathers
stretching fins across the beach

you lot always stretch beyond your
reach, building castles on sand

pouring concrete on soil
thinking yousef is safe

stacking borders in brick and ink like
time ain't teeth to man-

made structures. Do not measure me
in buckets and pots

I measure in erosion
measure me in patience

measure me in vengeance
You have never seen my final form

child, I was an ocean
long before you were born

what are you but another man
claiming what he doesn't understand

a baby trying to name his mother
ask my children for some wisdom

you should listen
when they tell you

keep your distance
keep your distance

wretched tourist
keep your offering

Only death and damp for you, here
do not test me, foreigner

River don't know you
River don't like you
River don't recognise you
river said watch how you wade

Bone and Soil (Shabaka Hutchings Remix).
Carmichael, Chelsea. Idehen, Joshua. Hutchings, Shabaka.
Native Rebel, 2022

bleach

BLEACH TILL BEIGE IS YOUR HOMETOWN'S
FLAG AND YOUR SHAME IS HANDSOME TIL
MY MOBILE PHONE IS A HANDGUN UNTIL
YOU'RE A JAPANESE WOMAN TRAPPED IN
THE BODY OF SCARLETT JOHANSSON
BLEACH TIL UR GARGLING YES MASSA
DINDU NUFFIN ON DAILY MAIL'S COMMENT
PAGE BLEACH UNTIL JESUS' EYES ARE BLUE
AND YOU ARE BEACH BLONDE COCONUT
BREASTED CHEWING STICK WAISTED FLAT
WHITE BELLIED PUKE DOG SKINNED AND
ON THE COVER OF MODERN STANDARDS
DOT COM BLEACH TIL YOU SMELL LIKE THE
WHITE MAN DOES WHEN HE'S WEARING A
3 PIECE UNDER NIGERIAN SUN AND YOUR
FLAT NEVER SMELLS OF CURRY AND YOUR
LAUGHTER IS UNTHREATENING AND YOUR
DEMEANOR IS BUTTERLESS BREAD AND
YOUR MELANIN IS DIPPING SAUCE BLEACH
TIL YOU CAN'T SEE YOUR REFLECTION IN
YOUR MOTHER'S BEDROOM MIRROR AND
YOUR FAMILY TREE IS AN UNASSEMBLED
FLATPACK BLEACH UNTIL YOUR DREAMS
COME WITH FIVE SECOND UNSKIPPABLE ADS
AND YOUR NIGHTMARES SERVE YOU BED
AND BREXIT BLEACH TIL GOD CAN'T SPOT
YOUR NEGRO SPIRIT AMONG THE CLOUDS

AND GOD CAN'T CONCEIVE OF YOU AND
YOU CAN'T CONCEIVE OF GOD AND NOW
GOD DOESN'T EXIST AND YOUR PARENTS
ARE UPSET NOW LOOK WHAT YOU DONE
BLEACH TIL U R RADIO FRIENDLY BLEACH
TIL YOU'RE TWERKING WITH BOBBIES AT
CARNIVAL BLEACH TIL YOUR SON'S FIRST
WORDS ARE DON'T SHOOT BLEACH TIL HA
HA HA HA YOU GET IT NOW IT IS THE RAPE
IN THE JOKE THAT IS FUNNY BLEACH TIL YOU
THINK YOU'RE ONE OF THEM BUT YOU AIN'T
ALT RIGHT JUST ALT WHITE WOMP WOMP
GONNA NEED MORE BLEACH TIL YOU BLEED
TORY BLUE BLEACH TIL LET'S BE HONEST
WHAT OPTIONS DO YOU HAVE LEFT AT THIS
POINT?

YOUR QUEEN IS A REPTILE

Your Queen considers herself our better; by right of blood, by way of lineage, by grace of conquest, by the confidence of tradition. Your Queen asserts this message through her crown, her church, her parliament, her loyal subjects, her wealth, her relationship with the media and the British empire, who in turn celebrate her lifestyle, her fashion, her cuisine and her culture. Your Queen is financed by our taxes, which in turn validate the injustice of class and race based discrimination, in this here Great Britain: that some are born superior, and deserve more because of where they're from, or who they worship, or who they love, or who their parents are. *Your Queen is not our queen. She does not see us as human.*

We the immigrants, we the children of immigrants, we the diaspora, we the descendants of the colonised; we claim our right to question your obsolete systems, your racist symbols, your monuments to genocide. We who built your palaces, we who paid blood into your banks, we who died in mines so your crown jewels may have the biggest diamonds. We claim our place at the table, and we say:

> Your history is not pure, your empire is not whole, your conscience is not clean, your money was printed in blood, your high horse is three legged and your royalty wears no clothes.

Your Queen is not our queen. She does not see us as human.

We know where we came from. We came on boats, on planes, with passports and on the back of trucks. We worked three jobs and sent the money back home. We brought our motherland to life in our kitchens, our bedrooms, our churches, our songs, our dance, our sex, our pidgin, our patois. We found pride and strength in sweat, death, life, tears and each other. We knew the system was rigged and the only path to freedom was for the system to burn. *Your Queen is not our queen. She does not see us as human.*

We see ourselves as human.

Our Queens walked among us. Our Queens led by action, by example, our Queens listened. Our Queens made bright futures out of cruel and unfair pasts. Our Queens cried and laughed with us. Our Queens knew they were just like us from the beginning, not just when it suited them.

Our Queens are just like us.
Your Queen Is A Reptile.

Your Queen Is A Reptile. Sons of Kemet.
Idehen, Joshua. Verve Label Group, 2018

DARK CLOUDS

Check me putting
the dark in corners
two fingers at Churchill

Sunday find me in
your church, still

Loudest voice in the choir
open toe sandals, popped
up collar, holla

Check me bringing summer
to the borough
bringing rhythm to sorrow

Check me in a hoodie
Shokoto and boba
in my Sunday best and trainers
street scholar, chirpsing
on your sons and daughters

Two wheelies in your luxury flats
spray tan on your welcome mats

Check me in your parliament
360 degree turning necks

Check me disrespecting your borders
check me taking no orders
buccaneer in her majesty's waters

Ink black stain. Throw Britain
in the wash, in the end
I remain

dark clouds
dark clouds stretch out forever
tomorrow is bound to be better

Dark Clouds. Marc, Ben. Idehen, Joshua.
Glass Effect. Innovative Leisure, 2022

A WANT (RIOTS 2011)

To know you're in safe hands. Whether you utter a bang
or a whimper you'll be heard in this wasteland. To believe
in the due process; for law men and young men on either
side of the fence to regard each other as something other
than suspect.

To approach your child's killer and get respect
a few choice words to clear the unrest. To get
no brushes to the side, no casual disregard
no feeling so chewed up by the wolf in your chest
you're howling.

To say fuck it. Brush aside all notions of justice. Make
good the entrance for vengeance.

To be surrounded by strangers, united in a wordless
statement,

How frightening, having this much presence.

To belong to something bigger than a queue; wash your
grievances in the dark, a horde to your sides and back. To
hurt your home so badly the world knows you're alive. To
set something alight. To face down the law for a night. Go
ahead, put your lips to mob power and sip, big like Caesar;
roam on road, stride. To Hulk smash, mad dash, grab cash
cuz you're no fool, bruh, just brave, just foolish, let's face it:
no one raids the pirate ship and leaves the booty.

To be part of a movement, a moment, do you want in?
To hear the tales in a tongue you speak, have you seen all
the ting that I did, bruv, do you know all the stuff that I
got? DUDE, you want in? Meet up at Croydon let's have
a dance. You only live once, and you want things so much
because you've been told to. To be possessed by possessions.
To answer all the ads, window-shop and follow through,
buy in without buying in. You know the lottery's rigged.
You too deserve the best things. They taught us everything
in this city can be taken if you want it enough.

Everybody wants here.

I want it to end.
Make amends.
I want to care more
for people than
property. I want the
country to heal
properly, Failing that,
I want to move to
where the leaders
aren't complete dicks.
I want to know I'm in
safe hands.

My Queen Is Doreen Lawrence. Sons of Kemet.
Idehen, Joshua. *Your Queen Is A Reptile.*
Verve Label Group, 2018

Anyway / things are bad / the phone
lines are dead / the road is dark
and the wolf is a cop / the devil
don't rest / is it even a protest if
your oppressor lets you march / the rot
is settling in / but
understand this / my spirit
is not for kettling

 **Kill the Bill (My Spirit Is Not
For Kettling).** Idehen, Joshua.
Kill the Bill EP. Optimo Music
Digital Danceforce, 2022

LOCUSTS

Locusts being locusts
singing cricket in the cornfield
late at night

Binge-watching the end of days
Scratching out in the final hours
at least it wasn't woke

Selling wingspan for
ad space

Filling
your timeline with goatse

Dragged
kicking into the
down, screaming *do you know*
who I am? Then begging for quarter,
then silence, then *no, leave me here,*
this is where I belong

Locusts
cutting out the middle
man, eating money raw,
puking *it was worthless before I got here*

Locusts co-opting the ok sign
buying land in the sunken place

If we build it, blacks will come.

Locusts laughing, watching you
count the votes
on their way to the armoury

Locusts with five twitter accounts
two for climate action, two against
one undecided

Adding autotune to
genocide

Blaming crickets
for the famine
hashtagging gun victims
#areyoutriggeredyet?

Locusts demanding you unblock
and debate
them, you coward.

THE WORLD ACCORDING TO YOUR MUM DOING THE WASHING

Capitalism:

Your mum does the washing. You pay her a pound. You get her to do your mate's washing. Your mate pays you £50.

Communism:

Your mum does the washing. You do the washing. Every night you salute a photo of your dad.

Socialism:

Your mum does the washing. You do the cooking. Everyone is happy in theory.

Fascism:

Your mum does the washing under the threat of violence.

Nazism:

Your mum does the washing. You gas the laundry room.

Feudalism:

Your mum does the washing and pays you tax.

Liberalism:

You watch your mum do the washing and feel really really bad. 'Something must be done,' you say.

Libertarianism:

Your mum does the washing. You believe you did it.

Religion:

Your mum does the washing. You thank god.

Atheism:

Your mum does the washing. You make a YouTube video demanding peer reviewed evidence she did, in fact, do the washing.

Misogyny:

You hate your mum whether or not she does the washing.

Patriarchy:

Your mum doesn't exist. The washing is mysteriously done.

Matriarchy:

Your mum does the washing. You do the cooking. You are really happy pulling your weight in the house.

Feminism:

Your mum insists you grow up and do your own washing.

White feminism:

Your mum hires a woman of colour to do the washing.

Male feminism:

That one time you did the washing, you told everyone about it and you blogged about it, bragged about it, took a selfie, Insta story, went on Oprah, won an Oscar, went on Fortnite, did a dance. You're an ally, hashtag me too.

Hollywoodism:

You are Colin Farrell. Your mum is Angelina Jolie. There is sexual tension. An unnamed black maid does the washing.

Cultural appropriation-ism:

While your mum does the washing, you steal her dirty clothes and mimic her in public. Public gives you money.

Colonialism:

You barge into mum's room. Claim you 'discovered' her room. Dump your dirty clothes on the floor.

Americanism:

Your mum does the washing. It's in the constitution. END OF DISCUSSION.

Mansplaining:

Your mum does the washing. You tell her how best to do the washing. You have never done the washing.

Misandry:

That one time your mum refused to do the washing is proof she hates you.

Egalitarianism:

You did the washing. Everything is equal now. No one needs feminism any more.

Hip Hop:

Everyday I'm hustling/ every day I'm hustling/ when I bring the basket/ mama put the washing in.

Hotepism:

Black women are queens. The white man is a devil. The black race must open their eyes. Mum does the washing.

Narcissism:

You look good in the clothes your mum washed.

Surrealism:

The washing does your mum.

BLACK SAYS

Black is tired.
Black's eyes
vacant, Black's arms
leaden, Black's tongue
can't taste shit, Black's
stomach cannot compress
Death

Black would like
to state: Black is not
a beast of myth, slain
in a fable, recounted
on a roundtable by *brave*
blue-collar men

Black has demands.
Black demands baton-
proof bones and bullet-
resistant skin

Black wrote an article:
500 years that prove
state-approved
lynchings should go
the way of dubstep

Black thinks no
person that trigger-
eager deserves a badge,
much less a gun

Black knows one day
their hands will go
up and their lips will be
pinned but their shadow
might reach for something
that's not there and that
will be enough

Black says keep your reparations,
just let Black reach
the other side of the street,
just let Black reach for the last
Skittles sweet, just let Black
reach into Black's own
car, Black's own lung

Black doesn't want
their young ones seeing
their fathers die on YouTube,
pausing halfway to keep
them alive.

Black says
it's always
been like this.
It's you who's late
to woke

Black has seen your grin,
your grin is a cutlass flag
Black's hands are bleeding
from gripping the knife

edge you offered on your side
of the handshake

Go write your thoughts
and prayers on paper,
fling it at the moon,
see what that'll do

You call for calm,
for peace, like a sacrifice
on a mountain's peak, doesn't
end palava. Calm
at the top, underneath's
still lava. Black

is angry now

Black is in pain. Black's
nerves are fireflies dancing
with grief, a &@$%
trapped in a bracket
a sentence too intense
for one full stop. Black's
pain needs three...
fading into Black
sitting in the dark
with the lights off
candles out Black
knows you commiserate
Black knows
you sympathise

Black says
you don't
understand Black
says you
cannot
compare Black
says this
pain is
too pepper Black
says you
cannot digest Black
says how
can you relate?

When these Black
lips are this full and these Black
knees are this ashy and this Black
voice is this loud and these Black
cheeks are this round and this Black
skin is this proud and this Black
skin is this cocoa-butter shiny and
this Black praise is dance! this Black
sorrow is dance! this Black
struggle is dance! this Black
hair is nappy and balding
and weaved and braided
and thick it's so thick it's so
thick it's so thick it's so thick it's
so long, octopus legs stretching over
skies blotting out the sun inking
on the cotton and the cocaine and

now Black's emotions are
a hurricane

and now Black's emoting
from Everest

Black says Black has
tried everything

Black has jived with both
hands, Black has breastfed
your children, Black has pulled
their pants up, Black has written
poetry in English
Black has laughed at your stupid
stupid, stupid jokes, Black
has eaten your terrible
rendition of jollof, Black has
stiffened its tongue
and now Black wants
to know what else Black can do?

Black is desperate now

Black's brought all their children
to the parking lot, its treasures
to the auction block. Black
is willing to negotiate

Black says give
Black some dignity

and Black will
give you twerking

Black knows you love
hip hop. Black will
swap hip hop for a chance
to live on their feet. Black
says let Black have a safe
space with all of their friends
and family and they'll let you have
first place in the 100m final,
get the Williams sisters to give back
all their trophies

Black wants you to know
nothing is off
the table

Black
would do anything
for their humanity

Just let black be.
Black says,
just let black be.

Black. Sons of Kemet. Idehen, Joshua.
Black to the Future. Impulse! 2021

TAKE ME THERE
(FOR PASSING CLOUDS)

Take me there, take me there
to the ends of the earth
just take me there.
So unusual, so nice
dotted tees and crossed eyes
spilt drinks, crossed wires
black bags and tainted ice
warehouse party paradise
my soul flies, paraglides
sweatshirt paradox
hope and lust in plastic cups
skinny girls acting tough
broken nose, laugh it off
don't know your name, let's keep in touch
angel wings in hooded tops
nicotine, halo ring, what further
madness, what future scenes?
shooting stars and loaded stares. Tell me
your name and twirl your hair
chat up lines in stairwells
that look of yours will stir me well
sign your name on a paper flag
tell me how you chipped your tooth
boiler room, touch the roof
feel the bass, can hardly move
refugees on dance floor
said she came from Darfur

bare feet on asphalt
high heels in mud huts
on the move; she can't stop
got on a boat and cast off

bad times? had lots

Darkness

take me there

Take Me There. Benin City.
Last Night. Moshi Moshi Records, 2018

ALL SMOKE AND NO FIRE, OR, LOOK WHAT THEY'VE DONE TO MY POOR HACKNEY

It's ten past twelve and the doorman's giving me grief
brand new bar where the job-centre used to be
you could spend more in a night
than most round here will earn in a week
said the doorman, *isn't there somewhere you have to be?*

Sorry mate, no hats, no trainers
could you move to the side of the pavement?

> *What about that dude, he's got trainers?*
> *I live on Well Street, bruv, we're neighbours*

No need to yell
you're terrifying the clientele
I don't make the rules, it can't be helped
you can't stay here, you got to go

—

there's a fire-sale on the home-front
Hackney's just got a nose job
the local pub's now a clothes shop
I need to piss, cant afford a pot

who's got the price for this culture?
who got the time for us poor sort?

dunno what you were expecting bro
we own the lease, you pay the rent

I swear you think I am daft bruv
you must be having a laff bruv
your shoes are in my gaff bruv
your croissant is in my cafe bruv
your flat is in my dancehall
your parking in my market
this borough is where I'm from, is all I know
If I can't stay here, where will I go?

Will this be the day, the day that I go down for good
all smoke and no fire, electric shock with no wire
will this be the day, the day that I go down for good
sharks in this water, all dark in my corner

All Smoke, No Fire. Benin City.
Last Night. Moshi Moshi Records, 2018

CURTAIN ROAD, 2015

Outside the Fox & Hound
you can hear them howl

city graffiti: keep calm
burn it down

life's all good save that
itch on my heel

London is this open wound
that will never heal, and

sometimes it's funny
the same words, once tailored
to his heart, made him sing and yearn

now hang in the air
smarting his ears
stinging his eyes
bringing him
down to tears

This Is LDN III. Benin City.
Last Night. Moshi Moshi Records, 2018

CURTAIN ROAD, 2017

I seen grief and I seen kindness
London at its worst and the finest
now Curtain Road is quiet
I got beer stains on my T-Shirt
I got luck on top of my Guinness
got friends amongst these sinners
I got love to the point of spillage
bright lights, the night is done
now it's back to the ho-hum
yeah, back to the humdrum
one more rat in the race; it's a long run
it's a regular job, with moderate prospects
heavy head, a mouth full of wotsits
on a cold sofa, telly and what's on
I stress over what comes next
tell myself *stay cool and positive, yeah*

Not The End. Benin City.
Last Night. Moshi Moshi Records, 2018

A DUMB CONVERSATION ABOUT IMMIGRATION AT A WAREHOUSE PARTY QUEUE

There are
people
dying to
get out of
the places
you want
to visit

GHOST NOTES
(closed down, 2019)

Tonight, Ghost Notes hosts
its last haunting
it's seven pm
venue opens eight
band's at nine
you can wait outside
by any of the surrounding
pop-ups
in the converted concrete
car park:
the table tennis dining tables or
the table-top football dining tables or
craft lager lounges with a DJ
spinning on a vinyl player sprouting
out of a vintage desk of draws
it all looks very cool, I swear

I meet Yomi
tell im I'm going Ghost Notes
tell im it'll be closed for good soon
tell im to come through
it's free. Come bear witness

He declines.
Who goes to a funeral if they don't have to?

But I'm here, still, gawking at the hearse.

GRENFELL

Living   in
LDN   is
a   hard
ship. Little
choice but
to   shuffle
into   a
match   box

ALL THE SAME

French kiss with the braces
played your song
and you feel your heart racing
and she downed that GnT
just to spit it in your face

saw everything as you wished it
blinked, it was gone in an instant
and the disco ball is
turning all the same

> *And we've all been here before*
> *we fell apart at our favourite song*
> *and it's such a shame*
> *and the disco ball is turning all the same*

in my corner of the world, you're the sun
you melt the dry ice in my lungs
nicotine on your tongue's what I'm fond of
we would make a great verse on a love song

and she said *don't get it twisted*
your heart ain't really that safe here
but your liver's gonna do just fine

And we've all been here before
we fell apart at our favourite song
and it's such a shame
and the world will keep on turning all the same, all the same

on the ceilings, circles dance
above drunken circumstance

she said she almost fell in love
I swear I almost caught her

All the Same. Idehen, Joshua.
Learn to Swim, a Mixtape. 2023

LOST IN THE CITY

It's obvious you don't get on
with this metropolis

The big smoke's
a big joke and you're the butt
of it

Not like before when you
were sure you'd fall in love
with it, eventually

Pity; the city
hates the optimist

You had your summer thing,
you had your summer fling. Now,
you feel the whistling, the winter
tightening the fist

The night is thick, octopus ink
friends and cash
keep mind out
the pits

but you're skint. Body
in a separate zone

City wears
loneliness like
nasty cologne

Nowadays
it's like the city's
fallen out with you,
the sky is frowning
like the city
wants to battle you,
you light a candle
and the city throws the dark
at you

Carry on, tho. Try not
to stumble.

> *You're not a part of this city*
> *It's not a part of you*
> *Been living here for years*
> *It's like you're passing through*
> *You're not a part of this city*
> *It's not a part of you*
> *Lost, here, lost in this capital*

Lost in the city
and it is lost to you

Scream all you
like. Be silenced
by the lights, dazzled
by the nightlife, drowning
in the pints

There's no need
to be yourself,
be anyone
you like

You could be
the city's bit of fun

Nighttime owl, daytime admin; star
of the now, has-been come morning

Not everyone
who grinds in the
city gets to shine

Many turn blurred
many turn blunt

Many aim for the stars,
get stuck in the gutter

You have
got to be acidic
to survive
the city's guts

Shouldn't you leave the city,
since you hate it this much? No, I can't
leave now, it promised so much

It has me by heart
it's got me by the crotch

The prize is so close
I can almost touch

I'm gonna make it
you can hang around

and watch. I'll be dazzling
in its limelight, I'll be
brilliant in its sights

I'll be a part of this city
part of it true and true

I've seen its ugliest
faces, soon I will see
it new

Lost / Early Mob / Your Coat. LV. Idehen, Joshua.
38 EP. Keysound Recordings, 2012

PRAYER FOR SAD TIMES
(PRESERVATION PRAYER)

I pray my
friends and their
friends stay alive
we fireworks
are due our Nov-
ember five
we have so much
loving to get back
to

UNFOLD

There's you down
in Dalston Nest. When
in doubt say yes
Friday night in
your Sunday best
Moon sits high in
the blue night's chest
Wash you clean of
all your stress. By
hook or crook you
will be blessed

Pass the club's
curtains your whole
body is energy
from your hair
follicles to your belly
full of KFC. House
rum, house coke,
house bubbly

There's you, in the low
end of the mix: club sweat
air, warm vibes, bright lights:
it's a hit. Strangers, smiling
faces, everyone on first name
basis. What's more holy than a
drop? Can't name it

There's you, giddy as
the molly takes hold
the crowd goes mad
the universe unfolds
Hands in the air
Sent word to the gods
and you got no answer
it's all in our hands now,
it's all in our hands now
It's all in our hands

 Unfold. Idehen, Joshua.
Learn to Swim, a Mixtape. 2023

ONE FINAL NOTE ON LONDON
(Strawberry Moons, 2005)

Nah, actually, that's it
no music singing, the sound is off
no more secrets, the lights are up
no good times left, all the clubs are shut

But you
you did the rounds, you tipped that cup
personal record of fifteen shots
strangers, lovers and fisticuffs
new friends made and in crowds lost
weren't you a handle weren't you a lot
bus ride singalongs wasn't it just
4am morning says that's enough
you're out in the cold and the daylight is bold
and you're alone with the last person in the world

Yourself.

STAY COOL, LEARN TO SWIM

Stay cool, learn to swim

> I only started learning last year
> and now, I'm forty two
> and if you already
> know how to swim? Good for you
> this is for the people behind you

Stay cool, learn to swim

> Nah, fam, you're not too heavy
> your bones are not too dense
> Pennywise was right
> in the end, everyone floats

Stay cool, learn to swim

> Your skin will thank you
> your mind will thank you
> and if there is blood in the water
> sharks will thank you

> Don't swim in the River Thames
> Nobody asked you to do that

Some things will always be true

The sun always sets in the west
right now is as good as it gets
Romeo and Juliet? tragic
time is wasted on worry
and everyone is made of pure
unadulterated magic
except for Boris Johnson

Trans men are men
trans women are women
some things by now should be a given

It looks worse when it's online

Facebook is not research no matter
the hours you spent on it
There are no solutions
at the bottom of a doomscroll
and you're never at your best
when looking at someone else's highlight reel

Time heals all wounds and makes new ones

But a hot shower will cure 99%
of bad vibes, truss me

You should be nice to yourself

You should be nice to people
except for nazis
no one should never be nice to Nazis

There are so many ways to be yourself

> Don't get lost in the options
> all the paper straws in the world
> won't save a single polar bear but
> making Amazon pay their proper taxes could

All your idols will let you down

> Except for Keanu Reeves
> cuz Keanu Reeves is perfect

> You don't have to like Pink Floyd
> You don't have to like Prince
> none of it is by force

> Every elder is a village
> but some villages are full of racists
> and are not worth the visit

Protect your peace

> Cherish your joints
> eat your fruits and vegetables
> and mind your business
> don't be afraid to dress
> like an idiot at least once
> in your life

Embrace your cringe

New York is nice but
you should try Benin City

If they won't let you join a union
start a mafia
the means you cannot seize
you should steal

If you love doing a thing, and
you're not hurting anyone or yourself,
do the thing. Don't let anybody stop you
doing the thing. If you love shoplifting
from department stores, do the thing
department stores aren't people

Sometimes the answer is to sleep on it

Sometimes you need to face it head on
sometimes it's scarier in your head
and when you stop running, you realise
the monster was a shadow all along

Your heart will be broken

and you will break hearts, and when
the dust settles in your spirit,
do not forget to forgive yourself

Call all the friends
you've fallen out with

tell them you miss them
dying right is overrated

That does not mean you should down
a bottle of Merlot and text
your former lover, nothing good
will come from that
Recognise the difference
between alone and lonely

More often than not you won't
resolve all loose ends, your life
isn't that kind of movie, it's more
of a rambling soap opera that'll
eventually run out of budget

I hope you get old

I hope when you get old
compassion is cool again
if you're lucky, one day you'll
wake up, and you'll be out of
the zeitgeist's eye. You won't
recognise the music, you'd rather
go to bed at ten. Your pleasures
will be gentler, movements slow
goalposts shifted, your former
burdens slightly lifted, and that
would be okay, it happens to
most of us

Maybe by then you'd have stayed cool
Maybe you'd could do something else
with your life

Like learn to swim.

Learn to Swim Part II. Idehen, Joshua.
Learn to Swim, a Mixtape. 2023

SOME THOUGHTS ON DEPRESSION

There is a road.
You have to cross this road.
If you do not, the night will drink you up.
You cannot cross this road
because this road is a freeway
and no one cares about the zebra crossings.
Everyone is telling you to cross this road.
Everyone is telling you the road is clear.
Everyone is saying you must not believe your eyes.
Everyone is saying you must not believe yourself.

MY LOVE (FOR LEONE ROSS)

My love is my love
No, I don't believe in
one love, my love is far
from lovely, trust me
my love speaks the language
of anguish fluently
where my feet won't beat
my love runs free. Downs pills
and whiskey, spits in public
starts barfights with itself
rides shotgun with a baseball bat
knocking out lamplights, is both knight
and dragon whispers
like a blunderbuss: charges in
never count the cost. My love,
strange, wondrous, greedy
never lies! Has its own truth
it remains truthful to. *Fuck You*
my love never compromises it
just decided a while ago no high
ground too high that it can't fall
for you. Every word of my love
inflects with you. It's not the buffest
but every muscle it flexes
for you my love squats
between two lungs full
of pride my love never
listens. There is a furnace

behind its smoke no storm
can diminish, my love
walked through customs
declaring itself damaged
goods. My love flies
with fins, unsurprised
when it soars and it stalls
and it falls and it crashes
and it burns, and gets back
on its stupid feet and does
the ting all over again. Amongst
the coins in the wishing well, my love
is the heaviest. My love is
its own venom, its own weapon
no method to its madness
no measure to the badness
you cannot unsteady its
steadfastness, black holes
across the galaxy, studying the dark
of my love, not a match to
my gravity, frankly my
love doesn't like your love

My love will not fuck
with your love my
love does not box with
mitten gloves. War
with my love get written
off more than you can chew
you've bitten off beware
my love does not care

if your love was there
before it
and yours is the purest
the surest, most deserving
my love will eat yours and
claim self-defense like
what the fuck did you expect
from something this far from perfect?

           this self-centred and this self-taught
              all its wounds are self wrought
         my love is nasty, feisty, vicious, envious, callous
       conniving, crazy, petty, cocky, friendly, twisted, bitter,
         and talkative and golden and black and weary and
       lonely and simple and childish, flaky and aching, and
                              my

love does not like coldplay
does not wonder
why the stars are yellow

My love rails against the rain
bruised heels, broken lips
my love is an alchemist
my love turns lead to dust
and hopes ur impressed wit it
that's my love
the bitterest pill
if you knew it like
I know it would
you love it, still?

My Love. Benin City. Fires in the Park.
Audio Doughnuts, 2013

ON DAD

This one's about me and my dad.

Two years ago the bonds we had began to sag.

He's across the sea, and recently he's been cross, reason
being I took a course in poetry. Where I'm from,
children are more than children: they're investments.
Investments suggest a path to profits. So when I told
him I would be chasing sonnets for a living…

*YOU WANT TO BE A WRITER, EH?! YOU ARE
GOING TO WASTE YOUR LIFE?!*

I'm not going to waste my life, dad-

SHUT UP!

Sorry dad.

This one's about my dad and me.

He's across the sea but at least an eve a month we have
a family meet. They begin with a family treat: fried rice,
fried plantain and very big pieces of very fried chicken.
Telly off, brother and I in the living room. Mother
walks in, harbinger of doom. Father is in her hand on
the phone, loudspeaker. She puts him in the middle.
Mate, forget Lewis Carroll. Five minutes with my dad

will turn Alice little.

And while I'm in the bollocking, my elder brother's
on the other end of the sofa. Faded singlet, half-tired
shoulders, look on a face like 'oh well'. He keeps a
mystery like Roswell, all talk, no telling, whenever my
parents ask he's quick on the selling like

AND WHAT ARE YOU DOING?!

Sound engineering

He's a pub DJ playing Britney Spears for seven pounds
an hour. But my parents don't care about that

*AT LEAST HE IS MAKING MONEY. YOU WANT
TO DIE POOR!*

dad, I'm not going to die poor

SHUT UP!

Sorry dad.

The dismissal of a parent I can't wish on my worst
enemy. I know he thinks, in his own way, he's doing me
a favour. I know my dad, I know him well; he carried
his weight. Sure, took a lot of risks, not too pleased
with his fate, and I think in me he saw the scheme to
set things straight. Where he's from, respect goes to the
oil, the bullet, and food on the plate and the pen don't

weigh much on those stakes.

The speaker phone's trembling, the treble of my dad's voice.

Mum's hush on the lip, T-shirt, leggings and slips. She nods away to whatever dad says, and the more violent his voice, the more movement her head makes. That's how they relate.

Don't get me wrong, we do get on, my dad and me.

Example: back in the day I played him that Eminem track, you know the one, *my name is, my name is.* My dad digs in his record collection, comes back with the track that track was originally sampled from.

I WAS YOUR AGE BEFORE YOU.
YOU WILL NEVER BE MY AGE BEFORE ME.

That's me and my dad: remix and original, sequel meets origin, and though I grew taller, could never overshadow him. 'Cept now I'm in my own lane. I try to explain to him, I see a path that's not so clear to him but to me every step leads to a true th-

SHUT UP!

sorry dad.

He says *there's no money in poetry*. It's all good having a fancy vocabulary but that'll never get you an audience with the bank or the tummy. *You're underestimating steady cash-in-hand, it's the bedrock many backbones stand. You can't build a family on backwards plans.*

I say he doesn't understand.

He says *shut up.*

I say *sorry.*

Dad talks, mother nods, brother's like 'oh well'ing. Six eves, six months, no budging. I'm not listening. He's not listening. We stop speaking.

Christmas evening.

No chicken, no rice, no phone.

Relatives gather when it really matters: times are great, times are grave.

Mother's draped in raven.

Brother's in the bedroom, welling.

Topic of the day, who's going to pay for the burial, ceremony, wake, the partying, *OH YES, he's got two sons. they'll provide, what careers are they in?*

Shit.

Heart has the tonic, but the pocket has no gin. All of
my dad's shut ups spin in my noggin. An uncle taps my
shoulder.

You're the writer one, are you?

Eyes on his sandals, *yes uncle.*

Hm.
Every time I met him he would always mention you.
You should write something for your dad.
Something good, something lengthy.

Yes sir.

untitled

They only know what
they've been told
and I'm not telling   ·

Two past seven
should I go for a
walk or play tekken?

decisions, decisions
and now it's eleven

block the noises
block those noises
don't know god
but my demons know me

Searching scriptures
for some wisdom

pray for strength
control forces

My reflection, I reject
Is that me or a forgery?
Is that me or a forgery?

Grey clouds stretching out til forever
tomorrow is bound to be better

Theme For Us. Scrimshire. Idehen, Joshua.
Wickham, Chip. Albert's Favourites, 2018

BROTHER

we have to find a better way
to get on top our hurting
the way we took our pain
and made a church of it
call it coping   call it worship
raise our voices   to the chorus
the way we took our pain
and fashioned it into a sonnet
recited at the summit of our damages

look at me! wicked and bad!
big and broad chested
the most twisted of the pretzels
proud of my poisons
ignoring all the seeping
shoving my true feelings
into corners for safe keeping

I don't have no weaknesses!
I don't show no weaknesses!

is this your masculinity
or your trauma speaking?

maybe you've said
unfortunate things
to yourself, like

it's too late! your heart
isn't in the right place
nobody wanna
see your face

but I'm telling you
brother, you are loved

you are valued
the winds behind you
are still strong

and I know you're hurting
everyone's hurting
and everyone's trying
so you must try

the sun still holds the sky
but we are running out of time
same old same old isn't
gonna fly my guy in fact
same old same old has been
the problem for a while I mean

what are you going to do?
with all of your weapons
when your hurting comes to you
as a song and you cannot
deny the melody
and you're undone by the words
and all you can do is hum?

ON DIASPORA

You'll find us on the benches of Pentecostal churches,
black shirts among the all whites. You'll find us in the
boys' bedroom upstairs at the wedding parties, playing
single player Street Fighter 2 Turbo all night. Oily faced
like plastic forks, amongst the other youngin like a pile
of chicken bones.

Those of us yet to see our father's grave, who need visas
to go back to the motherland, who are not on speaking
terms with our mother tongues but break bread with
pidgin, *yes, abi he fit speak am but e no sound right. Abi he
know the greeting he no dey bow right and him be oyimbo but
you know, not quite white.*

They won't let us forget that time we ate Eba and Okra
soup with a fork and knife. And like any middle child
we did our best to prove we belong. We learnt how to
start the generator when the house boy was away. We
learnt not to look the goat in the eye as we sketched
open its neck with a pen knife, our shiny Vaseline feet
pinning its legs. We drank pepper soup straight from the
bowl, one go, no spoon, no water and we ran with the
kids of mechanics and we fell and the earth roughed
our knees and we'd get up quick, quick and we'd mask
our stolen palm wine breath with Supermalt and we
ate the paw paws off the paw paw tree, even though
it was cursed by the witch at the end of the road, our

Christian bellies illiterate to pagan spells and we did not cry when all that sugar gave us stomach ache because tears were a British tradition, and pride was our father's wide compound.

Those of us born 'there', overseas.

Those of us told tales at Heathrow airport, how Akamu tastes like corn flakes if you add enough milk. Whose hearts beat twice when we hear of 'back home'. Whose hearts skip twice when we watch the world cup: Eagles for the qualifiers, Lions for the quarterfinals, sad times wherever our flag is pitched. Us British Nigerians. Us Naija Brits.

LAST TIME

Ladybirds line
the pavements
of the garden
applaud the spartans
as they approach
the flat in Dalston
feel the hi-hats
ring the doorbell
welcomed into
Marvin's yard
the biggest smiles
the open arms
we come bearing gifts
Carling by the carton?
mate I'm starvin!
we got pizzas,
we got lentils
the walls rumble,
from the bassline
of the jungle
instrumental
then Benji spits a 16
bruv, that's mental!
booze, greens
pass the lighters
pass the Lynx,
Calvin's starting a fire,

smoke alarm, he
means no harm
just a madness
4 safe lads,
4 game pads
and Halo
not even the Papal
could say no
the night is
soundtracked
by Kano
inside these walls
I'm never defeated
might get hype
never got heated
six pm the sun sets
just like it did before
it was just another
weekend with three friends
how could anyone have
known it was the last
one, the end?

Last Time. Idehen, Joshua. Dove Dixon, Katie
Learn to Swim, a Mixtape. 2023

FURTHER MORE, ON DEPRESSION

I know that you've been feeling less than perfect
You wanna throw your hand up in the air
give up give up give up –
you will make it thru the day of this I'm certain
somehow

Somehow. Idehen, Joshua. LV. Dorsett, Shanaz
2021

END OF THE LINE

The end of the night finds me sober
I see the back of yous, summer nights
colder. Lights come on, shadow casts
over, we head to the exit but not
shoulder to shoulder. We safe
lads, now lonely soldiers,
the crows fly out, not a
murder. Fat lady sang
could only make out
the cadence. It's ok.
We'll stay cool,
I'll on your
profile posts.
I miss us but
I won't
say it.

We were meant
to fly, my friends

End of the Line. Idehen, Joshua. McCleery, Jono
Learn to Swim, a Mixtape. 2023

THE NOD

I see brethren in a foreign land. We cross paths and exchange a nod. In this foreign space where our kinda pigment's scarce, I don't really care if brethren's from my ends or these ends; right now it's enough they exist. Cuz just this last hour, some random white man stopped me on my way, spoke to me in German. When I said *I don't understand*, he said *sorry, do you sell ganja?*

No one but my new brethren knows how mad that is.

A nod is not a thing taught to me, like a handshake or a courtesy. My first one was at an escalator, Helsinki. I was heading up, brethren was descending. We clocked each other, and I hadn't realised how alone I'd been, all this time.

In a mall of cutting looks, upon brethren's eyes I felt seen.

As brethren passed by, I would've said hi, but my pride wouldn't let me. Go for a hug, maybe a hi five, was scared brethren wouldn't get me. But they did a nod, without thinking I did a nod. That's how I knew we were safe.

All it takes is one nod, and Helsinki is my city, Berlin is my backyard, Sweden is my uncle's garden.

In another life, we would've shaken hands, maybe even hugged, taken seats at a random, politely hostile cafe, chuckled at the awkward interaction with the counter girl. Our masks off, our smiles loud and bad, our language uncoded, our laughter untethered to decorum, our voices unbothered, like we're in the belly of our mothers' kitchens. Like we live here.

Sometimes, there's a nod. Sometimes, there's not. Sometimes, they didn't see you. Sometimes, they don't see you. Sometimes you're the one who's lost. So it's a blessing whenever we clock eyes and the joy is on lock.

We keep it brief. One nod each, if you weren't looking you'd miss it type ting, a quick ting, a switch flick. And all the lights turn on where we stand and we are most safe.

How random, this meeting, here? Where the god of the land doesn't know our faces. And the law of the land's like *know your place.*

And yet, we're found each other.

How amazing is that?

Are we not alive?

Isn't that a beautiful thing?

ACKNOWLEDGEMENTS

You know when you had to tell all your classmates
in school what you did for your summer holiday? I
feel like that's this book, except... I guess I can say
something corny like 'this book is my presentation
in the school of life' but I'm here to tell you I
am exactly that level of corny: This book is my
presentation in the school of life. Anyway, I have way
too many people who have helped in one way or
another to craft, workshop and inspire the poems that
made it in here to thank, so I'm going to name a few
and apologise to whoever I forgot: Leone Ross, for
'My Love', Shabaka Hutchings, for Sons of Kemet/
The Comet Is Coming, LV, Benin City, Amy, my best
editor, Julia Hyltenstam, Yomi Ṣode, all the nights in
London where I honed my craft, in particular, the
Poetry Unplugged open mics, and Niall O'Sullivan,
who gave me my first paid set.